Introduction

Much is written these days on the subject of marriage, rearing children, and family life in general. But, by comparison, very little is available for the single person in our society. The widow or divorced person or the individual who has never been married often feels like the proverbial "fifth wheel on a wagon"—an "oddity," especially in the church.

It isn't uncommon for these people to be asked rather abruptly, "What's wrong with you?" Weird glances and cold shoulders don't help either.

But God has said some very special things to these very special people. In fact, it may surprise some of the marrieds to know that it is God's will for some *not* to be married. Amazing thought!

Hopefully, this little booklet will help inform and encourage . . . and even heal a few hurts within the ranks of our single friends. It is high time for many of us to realize there is nothing "wrong" with singleness.

Frankly, I know a few marrieds who wish they weren't! And that's a lot worse than being single.

Charles R. Swindoll

Singleness

Some time ago a cartoon appeared in a national periodical that caught my eye. The scene was very familiar. It was a busy traffic intersection. Cars were bumper to bumper in all four directions. Horns were honking. Engines were steaming over. Tempers were flaring. Impatience was written across the faces of irritated drivers. An intimidated pedestrian was standing all alone on the corner, looking across the street in disbelief at the sign. Instead of it reading the normal "Walk" or "Don't Walk," it flashed in bold red letters: "Good Luck."

I thought as I chuckled how very much like that is the world's counsel to those who are facing life's intersections, those who are standing at the crossroads. If you have ever sought the counsel of somebody that didn't know Jesus Christ and lived only the "me first" philosophy of today, you probably heard him say something like this, "Well, (humph!) I really don't know, but *good luck* in whatever choice you make." Great help when you're confused, right?

I am pleased to say that when we turn to God's Word (the Bible) at those threatening intersections in life, God doesn't flash a sign that says "Good Luck" or "I hope everything works out all right." God, as a matter of fact, can get very specific. And He may signal a certain direction to us that we don't want to hear. This is especially true as it relates to the domestic realm of life.

For example, some Christian man may come to God and say, "I have a great young lady I've fallen in love with, Lord. She comes from solid roots, she's attractive, and she really loves me. Furthermore, we see things eye to eye. There's only one little problem—she doesn't accept the same Christ I accept. She's not a Christian. But I'm confident we can work that out."

God doesn't respond, "Well, good luck, fella." God simply says, "No, my answer for you is this: Do not marry her."

You see, God's answers are often not as we would expect. I've come to see in my few years in the Lord's family that His answers are, at times, very illogical according to human reasoning. They don't make good worldly sense, *but they are always right*. Always.

Happiness IS Being Single

In this booklet I want to address a particular segment in God's family we frequently overlook, unfortunately. I'm referring to those who are not married.

In many churches there are couples' retreats and family conferences. There is counsel for the marrieds and special attention directed to those couples rearing children . . . but *very* little is ever said to or about the people who are single. My counsel to you today is not going to be "good luck." As a matter of fact, I am going to let *God* do the counseling, because His counsel is trustworthy and wise. Quite frankly, it will have something for all of us, not just the unmarried.

If you have a Bible or a copy of the New Testament, locate 1 Corinthians, chapter 7. Four domestic types are addressed in this chapter. The first 24 verses are addressed to *married* persons, for the most part. When you get to verse 25, you come to Paul's words to the *unmarried*. And then in verses 36 through 38, Paul addresses those who are *parents* of the unmarried. In the last two verses, he says a few things to *widows*. Our interest in this booklet is directed toward verses 25 through 37, where God is speaking to those who are unmarried.

One main point is communicated in these verses. Let's get that in our minds first before we look at all the verses which suggest some benefits for remaining single. The main point of the passage is this: REMAINING UNMARRIED IS DESIRABLE, BUT IT ISN'T DEMANDED. Rather than singleness being considered an undesirable life style, God offers different counsel; namely, the single life is desirable, but He is not demanding it. Keep that in mind. As much as many of us who are married may have difficulty believing it, the bumper sticker on those cars may be more biblical than heretical: "Happiness is being single." Not always . . . but when it's as God has directed, it is true.

Four Benefits of Remaining Single

In verses 25 through 27 of 1 Corinthians 7, we are given the first benefit of remaining single. Look at verse 25.

> *Now concerning virgins I have no
> command of the Lord, but I give an
> opinion as one who by the mercy of the
> Lord is trustworthy.*

Before we go further we need to understand that comment. It means that the Lord Jesus Christ, in His earthly life, never gave instruction on this particular subject. But in the progress of divine, inerrant revelation, God has revealed to Paul new vistas of truth never before disclosed to man. What Paul calls his "opinion" is actually just as inspired as statements of Jesus Christ because, in the passing of time, these words have found their place in the inspired canon of Scripture. Please understand, therefore, that this is not just another man's human opinion, but rather new truth never before revealed but equally authoritative and reliable. Or, as Paul clearly states, it is "trustworthy."

And now look at verse 26 with me.

> *I think then that this is good in view of
> the present distress, that it is good for a
> man to remain as he is.*

Less Distress From a Hostile World

The first benefit of remaining single is that you will encounter less distress from a hostile world. That's what verse 26 is teaching. Let me call your attention to the words, "in view of the present distress." By remaining single, God promises that you will encounter less hostility, less distress, from this hostile world.

To illustrate the truth of this, turn to the book of Hebrews, chapter 11. I want you to notice a series of vivid examples of the world's distressing hostility against God's children. Hebrews 11 is, for the most part, a long list of great men and women of faith. When the writer gets to the end of the list, he conserves space by summarizing the great heroic deeds of people of faith by not giving a lot more names. Look at Hebrews 11:35.

Women received back their dead by resurrection; and others were tortured, not accepting their release, in order that they might obtain a better resurrection.

Notice the growing distress experienced by believers from a hostile world.

. . . others were tortured, not accepting their release, in order that they might obtain a better resurrection;
and others experienced mockings and scourgings, yes, also chains and imprisonment.
They were stoned, they were sawn in two, they were tempted, they were put to death with the sword; they went about in sheepskins, in goatskins, being destitute, afflicted, ill-treated
(men of whom the world was not worthy), wandering in deserts and mountains and caves and holes in the ground (Hebrews 11:35-38).

Did these people have lousy testimonies? No, verse 38 says they were men of whom "the world was not worthy." But that's the kind of treatment the world gave them. In some cases they lost their lives. In other cases they went through mockings and scourgings, and even more horrible, inhuman tortures.

Now look back to 1 Corinthians 7:26. That's part of "the present distress" Paul has in mind. If a person was to remain single, he would undergo all that alone. But if he was married, he would have to endure such horrors taking place with his loved ones, which would only *add to* his distress. That's Paul's point. If you remain single, then you can encounter such distress with less trauma, but if you marry and add to the relationship precious little children, you may live to witness their being tortured unmercifully. One man writes of the times in which Paul lived in graphic fashion.

> . . . *the barbarities exercised on the Christians were such as even excited the commiseration of the Romans themselves. Nero even refined upon cruelty, and contrived all manner of punishments for the Christians that the most infernal imagination could design. In particular, he had some sewed up in skins of wild beasts, and then worried by dogs until they expired; and others dressed in shirts made stiff with wax, fixed to axletrees, and set on fire in his gardens, in order to illuminate them. This persecution was general throughout the whole Roman Empire; but it rather increased than diminished the spirit of Christianity. In the course of it, St. Paul and St. Peter were martyred.*[1]

You say, "Well, what does that have to do with our day? Such terrible things don't happen."

I disagree. If you have read a few of the books that have been written in our generation about the torturous treatment of Christians behind the Iron and Bamboo Curtains, you will find occasions where married partners were in such agony they openly declared they wished they had never married. To witness such barbarity against their mates and children was almost unbearable.

Paul's point is a practical one. You will, because of the present distress, be wise to remain single. Even in our own land there are certain hostilities and distresses that a person can encounter simply because he's a Christian. It's difficult to bear those alone. When you marry and you add to the marriage the children that also must undergo the persecution, you find yourself increasingly more distressed because of such experiences.

Verse 27 of 1 Corinthians 7 is linked with those thoughts on distress. He says:

Are you bound to a wife? Do not seek to be released. Are you released from a wife? Do not seek a wife.

If there are distressing moments that come, don't think that breaking the marriage is God's plan. And will you also notice that he adds:

Are you released from a wife? Do not seek a wife.

He's not referring just to those who have been married and for whatever reason are no longer. The word that is used for "released" is a term that means loosed or freed, and it could include those who have never been bound in marriage. It has reference to someone who is simply unmarried, even a virgin. The point I want you to notice is the direct command, "Don't seek a wife!"

If you spend much time with the single groups, you know that a lot of time is spent doing just that. What? Seeking a mate! It's remarkable how motivated young people can be when it comes to attending certain colleges. It is amazing what reasons some have for going to certain functions. What's uppermost in many of their minds? Seeking a mate! But the Scripture says not to do that.

I can read your thinking: "But aren't we suppose to pursue a marriage partner?"

Let me ask *you* something. Does this verse say not to seek a wife or does it say something else? I know I'm walking on a touchy area . . . a tender spot with some of you who are terribly lonely. But, be honest, what does verse 27 say? Then, what should a single person do? I think it is rather clear and simple. You seek the Lord and let the Lord seek your mate.

Ouch! I can hear some respond, "Oh, I've heard that stuff before at Bible conferences . . . all those miraculous stories how a guy in Africa dreams of a girl in Spain and they mysteriously meet in Alaska. Aw, don't give me that old stuff!"

Now hold on! Who said it will work like that? That may happen—but it's usually not quite so extreme. All this verse is implying is: Put the Lord Jesus Christ in control of your singleness. Give Him top priority. Seek Him—not some possible or available mate.

"Wait on the Lord," Isaiah writes. In fact, he says when we do that, we will exchange our weakness for His strength. Listen to Isaiah 40:31.

Yet those who wait for the Lord
Will gain new strength;
They will mount up with wings
*   like eagles,*
They will run and not get tired,
They will walk and not become
*   weary.*

See the word "gain"? Other versions translate the word "renew." It means to twist. The Hebrew verb conveys the idea of weaving something around something else that's stronger. It suggests adding strength to the first fragile thread strand. When we wait, seeking the Lord, we experience a strengthening we never knew before. At those times we release our panic and we turn over to God all the things He has designed and can do so much better than we ever could.

Do I write to somebody who is on the raw edge of anxiety? You just cannot seem to get things worked out for yourself? That person won't get interested in you? He or she won't catch your hint? That's not your job, my friend. Remember, the Lord knows your needs better than you do. Back off and let Him work. Your singleness is known to Him.

Now, let's press on.

Fewer Difficulties on a Personal Basis

Verse 28 proceeds with the continuation of thought. But it adds a dimension single persons easily ignore in their loneliness. Read the verse carefully.

*But if you should marry, you have not
sinned; and if a virgin should marry, she
has not sinned. Yet such will have trouble
in this life, and I am trying to spare you.*

Get the message? It's saying (believe it or not)
that people who remain single may actually experience fewer difficulties on a personal basis.

*But if you should marry, you have not
sinned. . . .*

We can all sigh a breath of relief together—we
haven't sinned.

*. . . and if a virgin should marry, she has
not sinned.*

I want to show you something. Some people feel
there is absolutely no ground for remarriage. If
that is so, then to whom is the *first* part of verse
28 written? He addresses the *virgin* who has
never married in the *last* part. (I'm personally
convinced there are grounds for remarriage be-
sides that of widowhood, but that's another subject.) In this verse, he's addressing both—those
who have been married, but now are not . . . *and*
those who have never been married. If the Lord
is in the marriage, there certainly is not a
problem of sin. Yet, he adds:

*. . . such will have trouble in this life,
and I am trying to spare you.*

If you are single, you may be thinking, "There
is nothing worse than being single. Nothing!"

Well, I can assure you, there *is* something
worse. Much, much worse. And that's being
permanently married to one with whom you are
not fulfilled or compatible. I fully believe that
we've often gotten the cart before the horse. Suc-

cess in life consists not so much in marrying the person who will make you happy as in escaping the many who could make you miserable!

Of the many people who write us seeking help, encouragement, and direction from our staff of counselors, we have a continual stream of letters from those who are unhappily married. Very, very few notes come from those who are unhappily single.

Paul is saying that in view of the increased distress from a hostile world and in view of the fact that you are sure to have trouble in this life, it's better, it's more advantageous, to remain single.

Less Deterrence in Time Spent on Spiritual Matters

Let's observe the next three verses of 1 Corinthians 7.

> But this I say, brethren, the time has been shortened, so that from now on those who have wives should be as though they had none;
> and those who weep, as though they did not weep; and those who rejoice, as though they did not rejoice; and those who buy, as though they did not possess;
> and those who use the world, as though they did not make full use of it; for the form of this world is passing away.

These words are a bit difficult to explain. The key to the understanding of them is in the first part of verse 29 and the last part of verse 31. Let's put them together:

> . . . the time has been shortened . . .
> (verse 29a)

> *. . . the form of this world is passing*
> (verse 31b).

The brevity of time is being emphasized. In light of the brevity of time, marrying and being involved in the cultivation of a marriage can be, quite frankly, an unwise investment of your time if you are the type of person who genuinely desires to be committed to Jesus Christ 100 percent of your waking hours.

This is the third benefit you'll experience if you remain single. You marry, you will be deterred. I didn't say derailed. Nor did I say that it was sinful. I simply said what Paul is teaching. If you do not marry, you will discover that you do not have to face as many hindrances in the investment of your time in God's work. The way these verses are written, a person who consistently has his or her eyes on eternity is being described. There is a constancy of focus on the day Christ is returning. And so when he is with those who weep, it is as if he is not weeping. There isn't the time, as it were. He is with those that rejoice, and yet this person is one who does not rejoice. There is concentrated intensity of focus on spiritual things. That's the thought. It's the picture of a person who keeps before him the reality of the coming of Jesus Christ.

Paul's great desire is to have an elite band of men and women in society who are completely available to Christ's cause. Absolutely no reservations or resistance. Singleness helps that happen. As a single friend of mine once put it,

> *When you remain single, Chuck, all*
> *earthly relations hang loosely about you*
> *in light of Christ's soon coming. It's just you*

*and the Lord Jesus. So many more things
can be accomplished from a spiritual
point of view.*

Now, maybe I need to remind you again that it
is not carnal to be married. If you marry, it is ex-
pected by God that you invest time with your
partner. Cultivating a home takes time. Lots of
it! Paul's point is, however, that if you do *not* invest the time with a partner, think of all the available time you will have for the things of God.

I was going through my files recently and came
across something I didn't expect to find. It was a
journal that I kept while I was overseas in the
Marine Corps. At that time Cynthia and I had
been married for only a couple of years. We were
forced to be separated because the Marines
didn't allow wives to accompany their husbands
overseas. She stayed home while I spent eighteen
months in Okinawa and Japan. I kept an exten-
sive journal during those days. I was surprised to
read some goals that I had set at that time.

I remember many, many days in the military
when I had time on my hands. Some weeks I
committed to memory twenty verses of Scripture. In fact, one especially relaxed week, I set
aside thirty-seven verses in a chapter, which I
memorized. Honestly! Why, I looked at that
journal entry and did a double take! I had completely forgotten that kind of accomplishment
had been made. I was also involved in evangelis-
tic campaigns which we carried on in the streets
of Okinawa with some of the fellows who could
play musical instruments. I was sharing Christ
with other Christian servicemen with whom I
was working. Totally available. Free and ready.

Out there in the trenches of life, giving the gospel to the men in the Quonset hut where we lived and to the other guys on liberty. By God's grace several turned their lives over to Christ, and I was neck deep discipling them, without any interest, any concern, in domestic ties. That wasn't important. It wasn't that my wife was opposed to spiritual things, it's just that we were temporarily away from each other and the time normally spent with her (and later, our children) was not there to interrupt or hold me back.

That's what Paul is saying here. My single friend, consider the time factor God has given you! Ask yourself, "Is God keeping me single so that He can use me or send me to a place to serve Him that I could not go if I were married?" Perhaps He wants to use you in some missionary endeavor, some special area of service, some involvement in His work that you couldn't take on if you were married.

You see, we are often so short-sighted that we think only of what we are *not* enjoying, rather than what God may have for *His* glory . . . for our spiritual enrichment . . . and others. Think about that. No one ever challenged me as a single person with the investment of time while I was single. No one *ever* brought that up. No preacher ever made that statement in any sermon I heard. I think we miss the mark if all we say to the many who are single is that the ultimate in God's plan for all of them is *marriage*. No. The ultimate in God's plan is that you who are unmarried seek the Lord and listen to what He is saying to you. Your singleness could become one of the highest spiritual plateaus you have ever known in your life. Believe me, my "single days" in the Marines certainly were that for me. It can have a marked effect on the rest of your life. See what Paul says in verse 32?

But I want you to be free from concern.

This statement introduces the fourth and final benefit in remaining single.

Fewer Distractions in Your Vertical Relationship

Look at verse 32 through 35.

But I want you to be free from concern. One who is unmarried is concerned about the things of the Lord, how he may please the Lord;

but one who is married is concerned about the things of the world, how he may please his wife,

and his interests are divided. And the woman who is unmarried, and the virgin, is concerned about the things of the Lord, that she may be holy both in body and spirit; but one who is married is concerned about the things of the world, how she may please her husband.

And this I say for your own benefit; not to put a restraint upon you, but to promote what is seemly, and to secure undistracted devotion to the Lord.

Let me describe what Paul is saying.

One who is unmarried is concerned about the things of the Lord, how he may please the Lord

(Perhaps we could say "*should* be" concerned about spiritual things. It doesn't necessarily mean that it is true in every single person's life, obviously.)

. . . but one who is married is concerned about the things of the world, how he may please his wife.

(Again, he *should* be, but it is not always true.) The interests of people are divided. It doesn't say those interests are carnal or wrong. It says they are divided. *They have to be!* When we marry we accept as our responsibility the cultivation of a Christian home. You stay single, you haven't that involvement and so you can spend that time normally spent in the things of God. But being married divides those. Our energy is spent on other things. I love the way verse 35 reads.

And this I say for your own benefit; not to put a restraint upon you, but to promote what is seemly, and to secure undistracted devotion to the Lord.

This fourth benefit simply amplifies the third. You can enjoy fewer distractions in your vertical relationship. The third benefit has *time* in mind; the fourth has *relationship* in mind. It mentions "undistracted devotion to the Lord."

While I was at a Christian camp several years ago, I had the joy of leading a Bible study group. Most of it was delightful . . . but there was one disappointment. There was an individual in our group who had recently come to know Christ. This young wife and mother had become absolutely absorbed in the activities of the church. Her life was so completely changed and her new faith was so exhilirating to her that her husband and children were relatively unimportant. They weren't totally ignored, but, for sure, they were third and fourth places (or lower) on her priority list. And she was really growing in spiritual things, or so she thought.

Someone else was at the same camp. This individual was an extremely confused and resentful person. Guess who that person was? Right, *her husband.* She thought this was the thing to do. She considered herself virtually "married to the Lord." I was tempted to ask if she cooked for Him . . . and washed His clothes . . . and listened to His words . . . and all those other things wives do for their husbands. I didn't, but you get the point. Her problem was this—she was a married person living as though she were single.

What I want to do is give a balanced picture of what Paul is saying. He is not saying that one is right and one is wrong. He's saying that if you make the choice to marry, then the time spent *for* the Lord (your investment of time) and the time spent *with* the Lord (your vertical relationship) must be divided with the time spent with those on this earth. Show me a home that is happy and enjoying internal relationships that are fulfilling, happy, and healthy, and I'll show you a husband and a wife who invest a whole lot of time and energy in that home.

Now back to the other side. Verse 35 has a very blunt message to the singles. Those of us who are married cannot apply this as you can. Look at verse 35, especially if you are single. Paul says that he desires—

> . . . to promote what is seemly, and to secure undistracted devotion to the Lord.

It grieves me to see so many singles today who are distracted in their devotion to the Lord. Just not interested. Passive. Perhaps you have listened to us who are married and you have misunderstood. Maybe we've given you the wrong information. Maybe you're following only the strong sexual drive of your life and you think that the only thing that is going to satisfy is to find a mate. That's not the scene I find in this section of Scripture. I find a person here who is available to the Lord and can give undistracted devotion to Him. Some of you may be thinking, "That kind of person just doesn't exist outside a monastery. Red-blooded youth cannot coexist with such spiritual fervor."

I disagree. And I have an example to prove the point.

An Example Worth Remembering

My wife and I know an attractive, gifted young lady. She's into her 30s and (of all things!) she's still unmarried. But (of all things!) that doesn't bother our friend at all. She told me while she was visiting with our family recently: "You know, I've gotten to the place where this issue of my marriage is between the Lord and me, not between a fellow and me." And she added, "It is the most wonderful thing to be able to invest this time in several lives." She named one girl after another in whose life she is investing time and energy. It's beautiful! One of her key disciples is a gal who recently graduated from college, very gifted musically. She's decided to turn her attention to the possibility of vocational Christian service. Why? Because of our friend's counsel.

I could name at least a half dozen others whose lives are getting back on target because this lovely young woman has decided to capitalize on her singleness rather than resent it or rush out and ruin it with the wrong guy. She is now useful for the Lord. She's thanking God daily that she is available, complete in Him. Why, she's just as free as she could possibly be. She's totally available to what God has for her.

I came across an amazing letter that was written by a young communist to his girl friend, breaking off the relationship with her because of his devotion to the communist cause. The letter was given to her pastor, and somehow it fell into my hands. Remember the background as you read this young communist's words.

We communists have a high casualty rate. We're the ones who get shot and hung and ridiculed and fired from our jobs and in every other way made as uncomfortable as possible. A certain percentage of us get killed or imprisoned. We live in virtual poverty. We turn back to the party every penny we make above what is absolutely necessary to keep us alive. We communists do not have the time or the money for many movies or concerts or T-bone steaks or decent homes or new cars. We've been described as fanatics. We are fanatics. Our lives are dominated by one great overshadowing factor, the struggle for world communism. We have a philosophy of life which no amount of money could buy. We have a cause to fight for, a definite purpose in life. We subordinate our petty personal selves into a great movement of humanity. If our personal lives seem hard or our egos appear to

*suffer through subordination to the party,
we are adequately compensated by the
thought that each of us in his small way is
contributing to something new and true
and better for mankind. There is one thing
in which I am dead earnest about and
that is the communist cause. It is my life,
my business, my religion. It is my hobby,
my sweetheart, my wife, my mistress, my
bread, my meat. I work at it in the daytime
and I dream of it at night. Its hold on me
grows, not lessens, as time goes on. Therefore, I cannot carry on a relationship with
you any longer, no longer a love affair, not
even a conversation with others without
relating it to this force which drives and
guides my life. I evaluate books and
people and ideas and actions according to
how they affect this communist cause and
by their attitude toward it. I've already
been in jail because of my ideals, and, if
necessary, I'm ready to go before a firing
squad.*

That, my friend, is having undistracted devotion
to a cause.

A Challenge Worth Accepting

Do I address some single
person who has to admit he has been wasting his
energy in the wrong direction? Instead of reach-
ing meaningful goals that will count for eternity,
you've been in a holding pattern. You know, just
circling the field. Distracted in your devotion
and therefore pretty discouraged with your life.

I want to throw out a challenge to you who are
single. As I do so, please understand I have in

mind you who have never married or you who have been married but are no longer. For whatever reason, your situation is now that of a single person . . . one without a marriage partner. This challenge I have for you will come in the form of three simple words. Three "commands" from the Lord, through me, just for you.

Rejoice!

You do not need to wonder why you have missed the best. You *have* God's best. Since God is sovereignly in control, it's His call for you right now. It's not, "Some day when I'm married I will count for Christ." It is, "Since God has led me to be single, I will capitalize on the benefits that are mine to enjoy." Rejoice in the occasion that's provided for you.

Reverse!

Reverse the energy that you've been using up in the horizontal syndrome of panic and worry . . . and turn it to the vertical. You will be amazed at how good He is at finding you a mate *or* giving you satisfaction without a mate.

Relax!

Let's face it, a fellow is not going to be very interested in a woman who is sitting on the edge of her chair, biting her nails down to her knuckles, wondering when he's going to get with it. You tip your hand. And fellows, God's still in the business of finding mates. Yours may not be in Africa or Spain, yours may be very close to you. But, relax. Give all the controls of your life over to the Savior, my single friend. And as you relax, watch Him redirect your life toward others who could really use some things you have to offer.

My advice? Not "good luck," but rather *REJOICE, REVERSE, RELAX.*

I dare you.

> *Dear heavenly Father:*
>
> *Our confidence in You is strong and firm. We are thankful that our situation is no mystery to You. Calm our spirits with that thought. Show us how we can not only accept our single state, but flourish in it. There are unique difficulties we live with—misunderstanding, times of intense loneliness, distinct feelings of rejection, and very real temptations most people can't possibly imagine. But we are confident You will use even these troubles to mature our walk. We do so desire to glorify Your name and to minister to others in an authentic and meaningful manner. Encourage us by opening doors of opportunity, then make us sensitive to You and bold in faith as we step through those doors to serve others who need what we can provide.*
>
> *In the strong name of Christ. Amen.*

[1]William Byron Forbush, D.D., ed., *Foxe's Book of Martyrs* (Philadelphia, PA.: Universal Book and Bible House, 1926), p. 6.